GOD LOVES YOU

CELEBRATE GOD'S PERFECT LOVE FOR YOU

chartwell books

Quarto

This edition published in 2025 by Chartwell Books,
an imprint of The Quarto Group
142 West 36th Street, 4th Floor
New York, NY 10018 USA
T (212) 779-4972
www.Quarto.com

10 9 8 7 6 5 4 3 2 1
Chartwell titles are also available at discount for retail, wholesale, promotional, and bulk purchase. For details, contact the Special Sales Manager by email at specialsales@quarto.com or by mail at The Quarto Group, Attn: Special Sales Manager, 100 Cummings Center Suite 265D, Beverly, MA 01915, USA.

ISBN: 978-0-7858-4654-3

Publisher: Wendy Friedman
Publishing Director: Meredith Mennitt
Editor: Amanda Carestio
Designer: Angelika Piwowarczyk
All stock photos and design elements ©Shutterstock

Printed in China

CONTENTS

INTRODUCTION

It's normal, from time to time, to want proof that God loves us.

Let this collection of quotes, parables, and stories be that gentle reminder for you: a celebration of God's perfect love for you, even with your imperfections, faults, and failings. God's love is pure, powerful, and dynamic, filled with perfect grace, mercy, and forgiveness. And all of that is available to you.

Wherever you find yourself today, surrounded by love and joy or challenged by trying times within your life, may you find peace and comfort in these passages, parables, and stories. Immerse yourself in the messages of love, kindness, and joy. Use them to regain your strength, provide stability, and find healing. To know and accept these messages will provide your life with many blessings.

Chapter 1

God's Love

The nature of God's love for humanity is deep and powerful, vast and everlasting. His love is ever-present in our lives, even if we don't always realize it. Through His sacrifice and unconditional love, we have access to many blessings.

For God so loved the world that he gave his only begotten Son, that whoever believes in him should not perish but have everlasting life.

John 3:16

For I am persuaded, that neither death, nor life, nor angels, nor principalities, nor powers, nor things present, nor things to come, nor height, nor depth, nor any other creature, shall be able to separate us from the love of God, which is in Christ Jesus our Lord.

❖

Romans 8:38-39

May be able to comprehend with all saints what is the breadth, and length, and depth, and height; And to know the love of Christ, which passeth knowledge, that ye might be filled with all the fulness of God.

❖

Ephesians 3:18-19

We love him, because
he first loved us.

1 John 4:19

For the Lord is good; his
mercy is everlasting; and
his truth endureth to all
generations.

❖

Psalms 100:5

And we have known and believed the love that God has for us. God is love, and he who abides in love abides in God, and God in him.

1 John 4:16

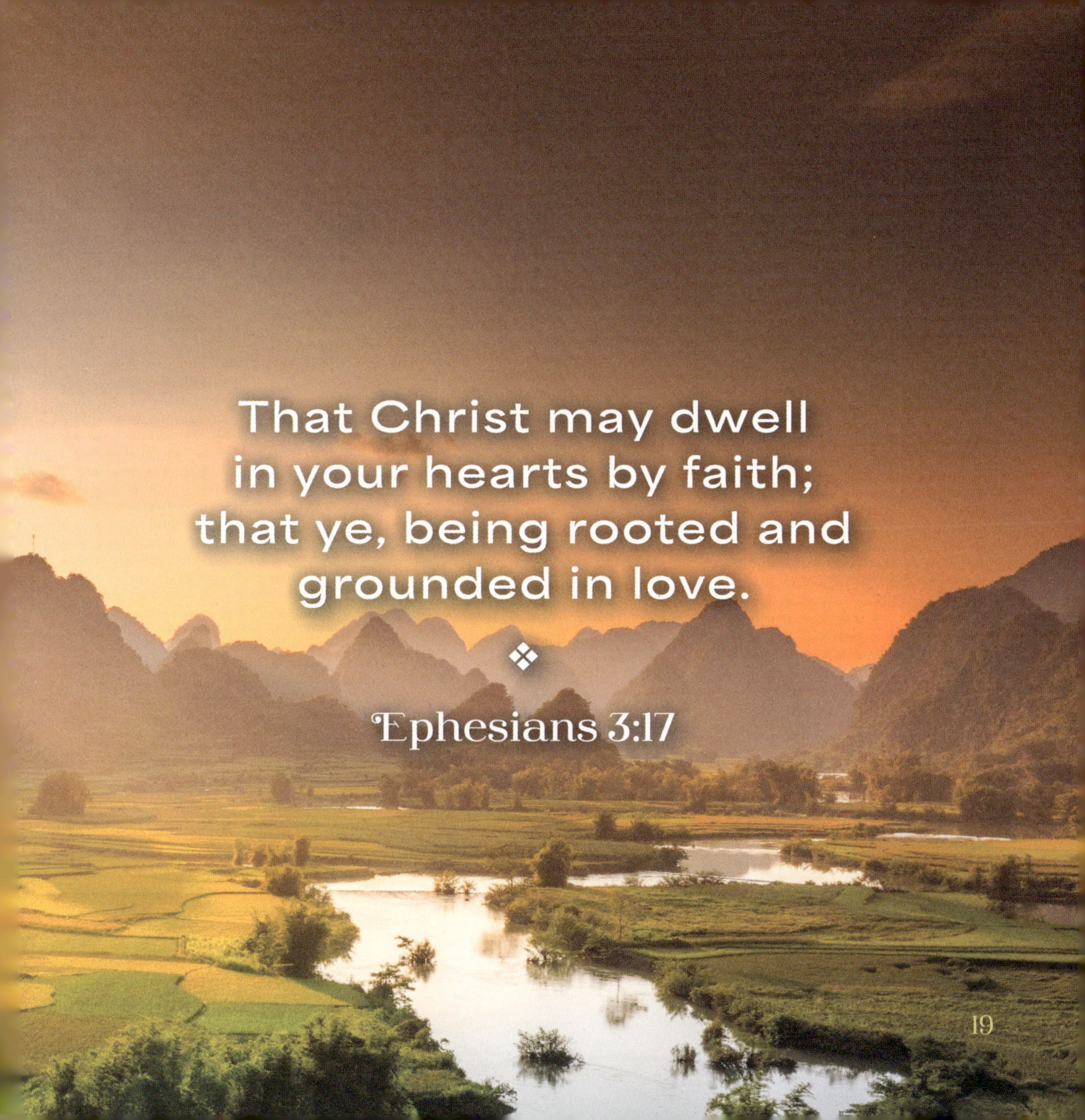

That Christ may dwell
in your hearts by faith;
that ye, being rooted and
grounded in love.

Ephesians 3:17

How excellent is thy loving kindness, O God! therefore the children of men put their trust under the shadow of thy wings.

❖

Psalms 36:7

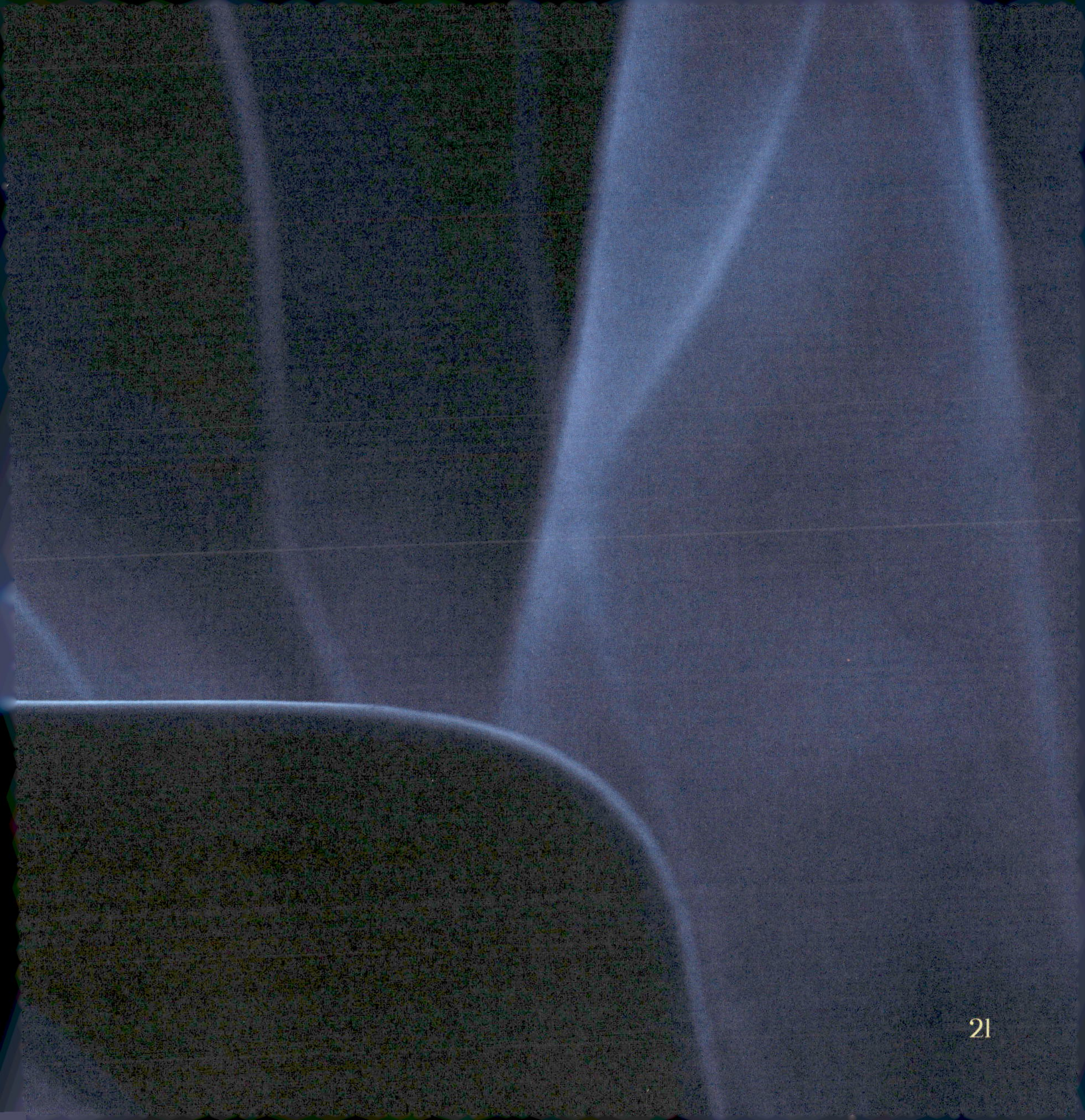

And the Lord direct your hearts into the love of God, and into the patient waiting for Christ.

❖

2 Thessalonians 3:5

God's Love and Jesus

Perhaps the most profound sacrifice God has made is that of his only son, Jesus, to save mankind from sin and ensure salvation. There's not a more selfless act or an act that proves God's love for us more.

For God so loved the world, that he gave his only begotten Son, that whosoever believeth in him should not perish, but have everlasting life.

John 3:16

This act reminds us of God's love for humanity, a central message to the biblical narrative. All God asks in return is for you to believe in the power of Christ, allow that power to transform you, and that you commit to your belief. The reward? Everlasting life in heaven.

Chapter 2

Joy & Happiness

Through God's perfect love, pure joy is available to humanity. Through faith, trust, and a personal relationship with God, we have access to true happiness, profound contentment, fulfillment, and more.

These things have I spoken unto you, that my joy might remain in you, and that your joy might be full.

John 15:11

Then he said unto them,
Go your way, eat the
fat, and drink the sweet,
and send portions unto
them for whom nothing
is prepared: for this day is
holy unto our Lord: neither
be ye sorry; for the joy of
the Lord is your strength.

❖

Nehemiah 8:10

Delight thyself also in the Lord: and he shall give thee the desires of thine heart.

❖

Psalms 37:4

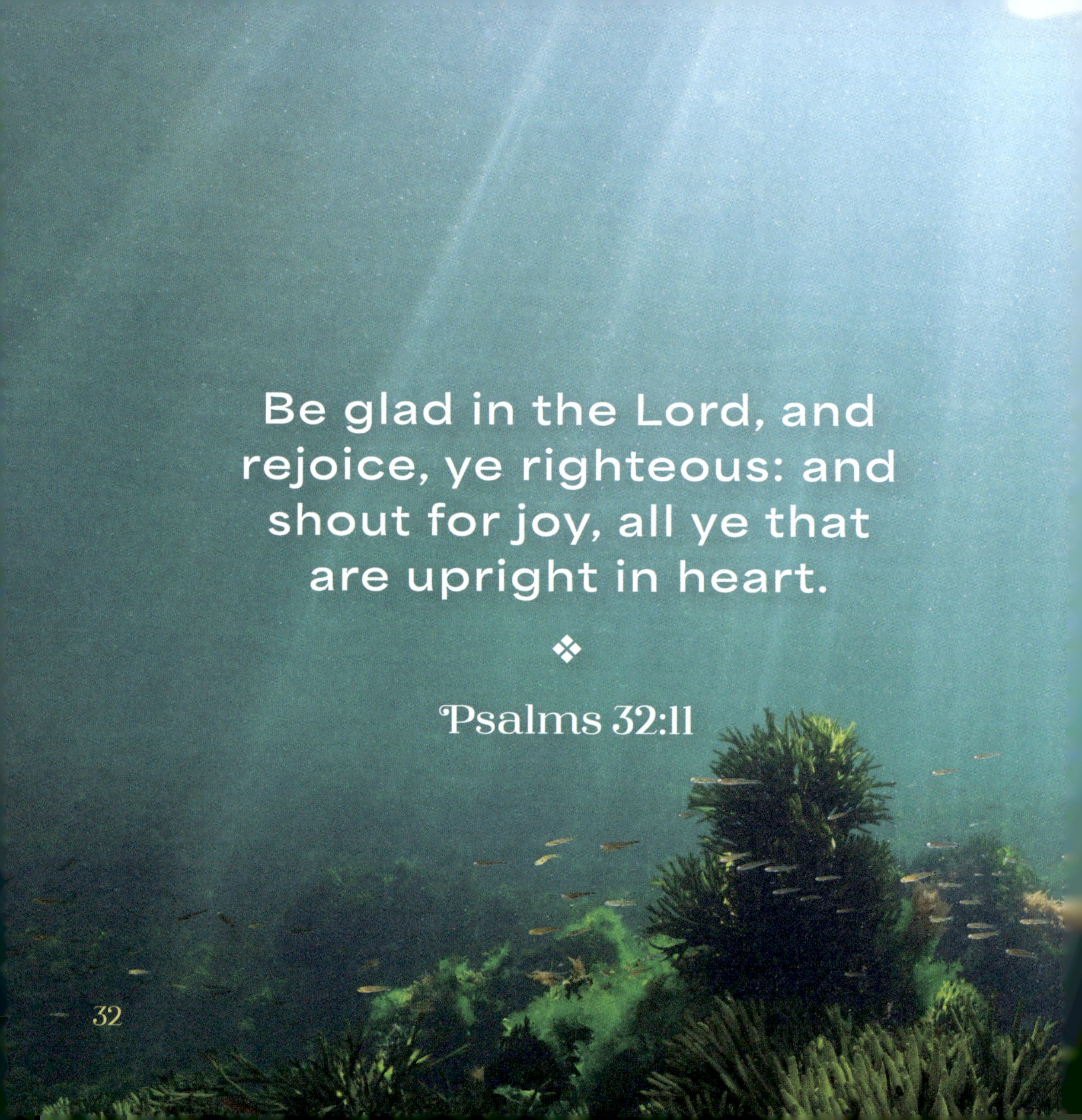

Be glad in the Lord, and rejoice, ye righteous: and shout for joy, all ye that are upright in heart.

Psalms 32:11

The Lord thy God in the
midst of thee is mighty;
he will save, he will rejoice
over thee with joy; he will
rest in his love, he will joy
over thee with singing.

Zephaniah 3:17

Thou hast turned for me my mourning into dancing: thou hast put off my sackcloth, and girded me with gladness.

Psalms 30:11

Then I commended mirth, because a man hath no better thing under the sun, than to eat, and to drink, and to be merry: for that shall abide with him of his labour the days of his life, which God giveth him under the sun.

Ecclesiastes 8:15

Now the God of hope fill
you with all joy and peace
in believing, that ye may
abound in hope, through
the power of the Holy
Ghost.

❖

Romans 15:13

Then shall the virgin rejoice in the dance, both young men and old together: for I will turn their mourning into joy, and will comfort them, and make them rejoice from their sorrow.

Jeremiah 31:13

A merry heart doeth good like a medicine: but a broken spirit drieth the bones.

Proverbs 17:22

Whom having not seen, ye love; in whom, though now ye see him not, yet believing, ye rejoice with joy unspeakable and full of glory.

1 Peter 1:8

God's Love and the Creation of Humanity

The story of Genesis is a reminder to appreciate all that we have and all that we've been given.

So God created man in his own image, in the image of God created he him; male and female created he them. And God blessed them, and God said unto them, Be fruitful, and multiply, and replenish the earth, and subdue it: and have dominion over the fish of the sea, and over the fowl of the air, and over every living thing that moveth upon the earth.

Genesis 1:27-28

Even with our faults, we are reminded to love ourselves as the work of God's hand, with grace and forgiveness. God's creation is very good, including us. And we are loved by the one that made us.

Chapter 3

Mercy & Forgiveness

Through God's love, redemption is possible. Whether you find yourself lost, astray, or in need of deep forgiveness, God will welcome you back in with open arms. And just as he has mercy for us, He asks that we should have mercy in our hearts for our fellow man.

For thou, Lord, art good, and ready to forgive; and plenteous in mercy unto all them that call upon thee.

Psalms 86:5

My soul hath them still in remembrance, and is humbled in me. This I recall to my mind, therefore have I hope. It is of the Lord's mercies that we are not consumed, because his compassions fail not. They are new every morning: great is thy faithfulness.

❖

Lamentations 3:20-23

But you, O Lord, are a God of compassion and mercy, slow to get angry and filled with unfailing love and faithfulness.

Psalms 86:15

But God, who is rich in mercy, for his great love wherewith he loved us, Even when we were dead in sins, hath quickened us together with Christ, (by grace ye are saved).

❖

Ephesians 2:4-5

For the mountains shall depart, and the hills be removed; but my kindness shall not depart from thee, neither shall the covenant of my peace be removed, saith the Lord that hath mercy on thee.

Isaiah 54:10

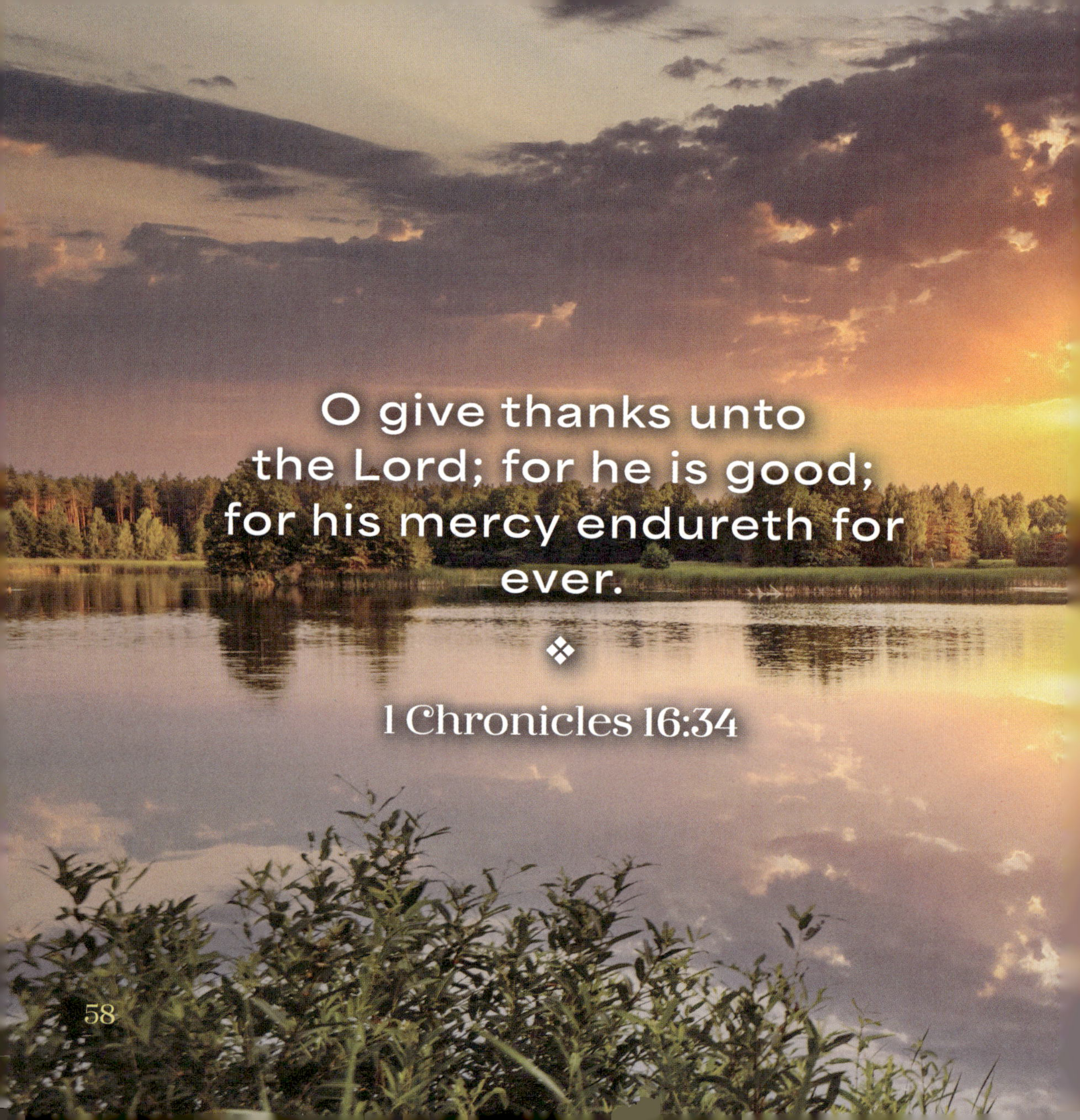

O give thanks unto the Lord; for he is good; for his mercy endureth for ever.

❖

1 Chronicles 16:34

Be ye therefore merciful,
as your Father also is
merciful.

❖

Luke 6:36

And be ye kind one to another, tenderhearted, forgiving one another, even as God for Christ's sake hath forgiven you.

❖

Ephesians 4:32

For thou, Lord, art good, and ready to forgive; and plenteous in mercy unto all them that call upon thee.

Psalms 86:5

And forgive us our sins; for we also forgive every one that is indebted to us. And lead us not into temptation; but deliver us from evil.

❖

Luke 11:4

Have mercy on me,
O God, according to
your unfailing love;
according to your great
compassion blot out my
transgressions.

Psalms 51:1

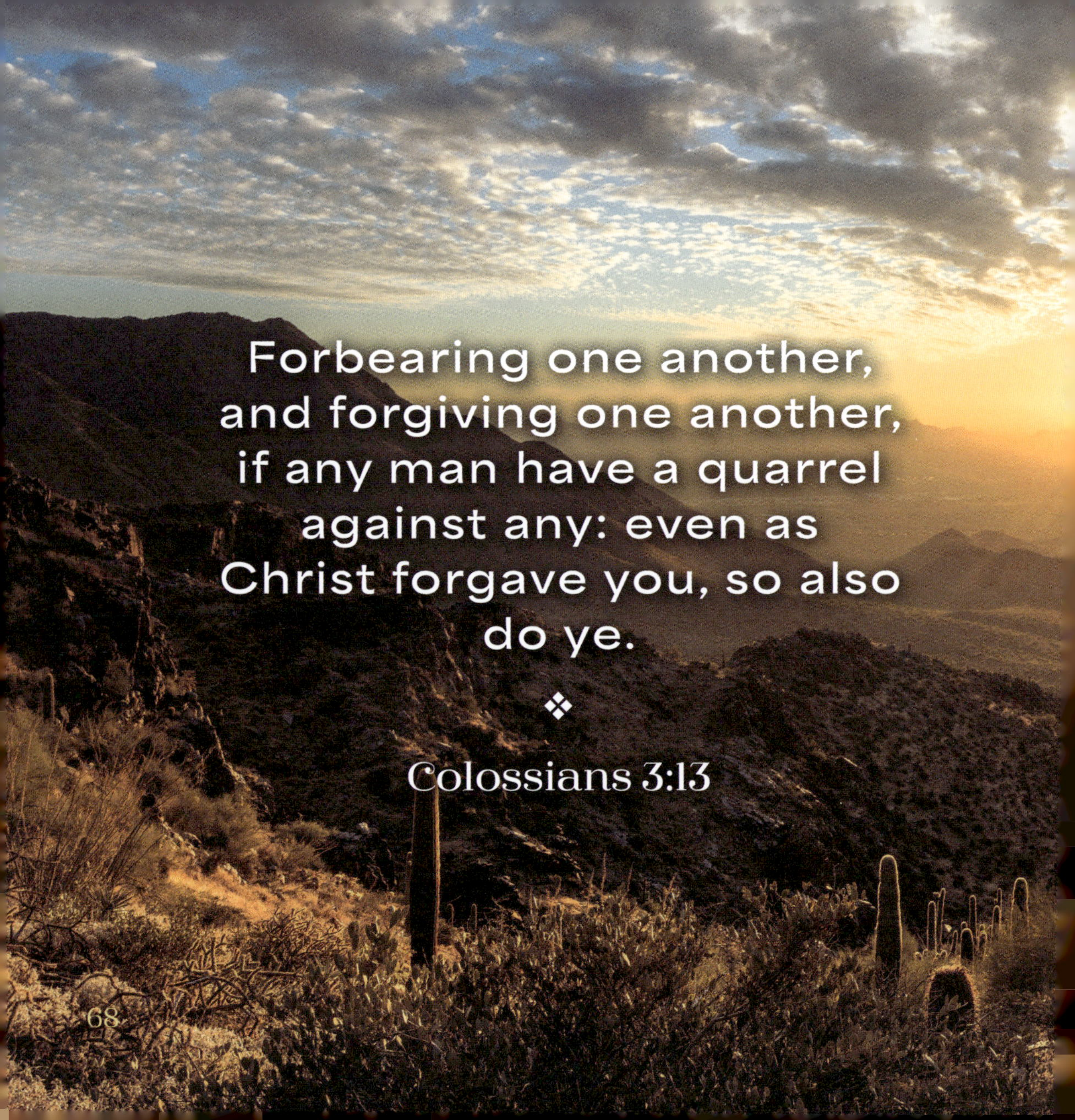

Forbearing one another,
and forgiving one another,
if any man have a quarrel
against any: even as
Christ forgave you, so also
do ye.

Colossians 3:13

Let us therefore come boldly unto the throne of grace, that we may obtain mercy, and find grace to help in time of need.

Hebrews 4:16

Blessed are the merciful: for they shall obtain mercy.

Matthew 5:7

If we confess our sins,
he is faithful and just to
forgive us our sins, and
to cleanse us from all
unrighteousness.

❖

1 John 1:9

The Parable of the Lost Sheep

The parable of the lost sheep appears in the Gospels of Matthew and Luke. This parable tells the story of a man with 100 sheep. When one goes missing, the shepherd leaves his flock of 99 sheep in order to find the missing sheep.

What man of you, having an hundred sheep, if he lose one of them, doth not leave the ninety and nine in the wilderness, and go after that which is lost, until he find it? And when he hath found it, he layeth it on his shoulders, rejoicing. And when he cometh home, he calleth together his friends and neighbors, saying unto them, Rejoice with me; for I have found my sheep which was lost. I say unto you, that likewise joy shall be in heaven over one sinner that repenteth, more than over ninety and nine just persons, which need no repentance.

Luke 15:3–7

This story reminds us that the kingdom of God is accessible to all, even sinners and those who have strayed from the path. It reinforces the idea of how precious each person is to God and how God will not let anyone perish.

Chapter 4

Healing & Peace

Perhaps one of the greatest blessings of God's love is his ability to provide healing and peace. Though you may still experience tribulation, within this deep healing love, you'll also find freedom from fear. And find promise of the ultimate peace: the kingdom of Heaven.

The Lord will give
strength unto his people;
the Lord will bless his
people with peace.

Psalms 29:11

These things I have spoken unto you, that in me ye might have peace. In the world ye shall have tribulation: but be of good cheer; I have overcome the world.

❖

John 16:33

He healeth the broken in heart, and bindeth up their wounds.

Psalms 147:3

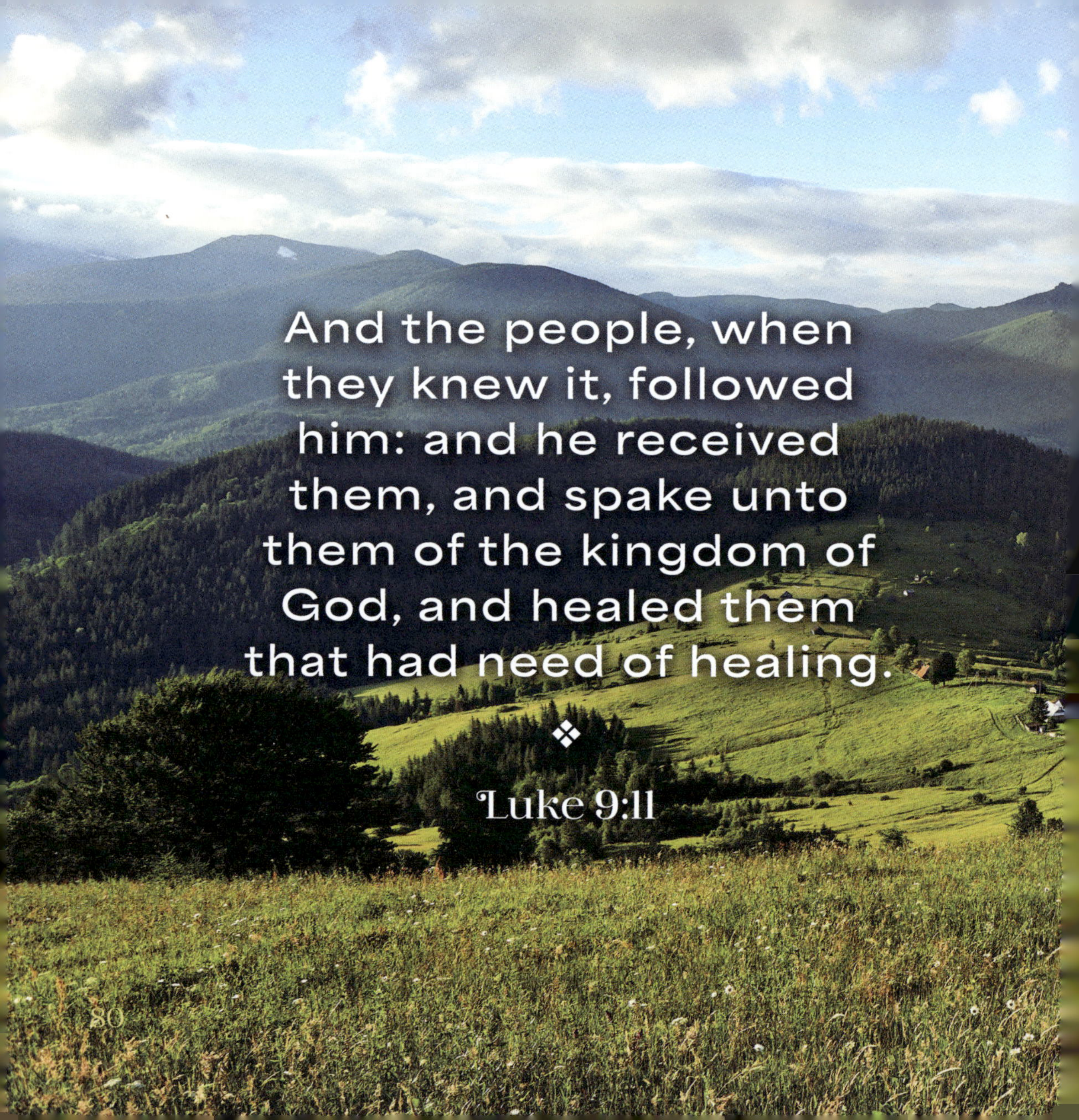

And the people, when they knew it, followed him: and he received them, and spake unto them of the kingdom of God, and healed them that had need of healing.

❖

Luke 9:11

Peace I leave with you, my peace I give unto you: not as the world giveth, give I unto you. Let not your heart be troubled, neither let it be afraid.

❖

John 14:27

The Lord bless thee, and keep thee: The Lord make his face shine upon thee, and be gracious unto thee: The Lord lift up his countenance upon thee, and give thee peace.

Numbers 6:24

Thou wilt keep him in
perfect peace, whose
mind is stayed on thee:
because he trusteth in
thee.

Isaiah 26:3

For God hath not given us the spirit of fear; but of power, and of love, and of a sound mind.

❖

2 Timothy 1:7

Blessed are they that mourn: for they shall be comforted.

❖

Matthew 5:4

Let not your heart be troubled: ye believe in God, believe also in me.

❖

John 14:1

The Lord shall fight for you, and ye shall hold your peace.

❖

Exodus 14:14

Then they cry unto the Lord in their trouble, and he saveth them out of their distresses. He sent his word, and healed them, and delivered them from their destructions.

Psalms 107:19-20

Beloved, I wish above
all things that thou
mayest prosper and be in
health, even as thy soul
prospereth.

3 John 1:2

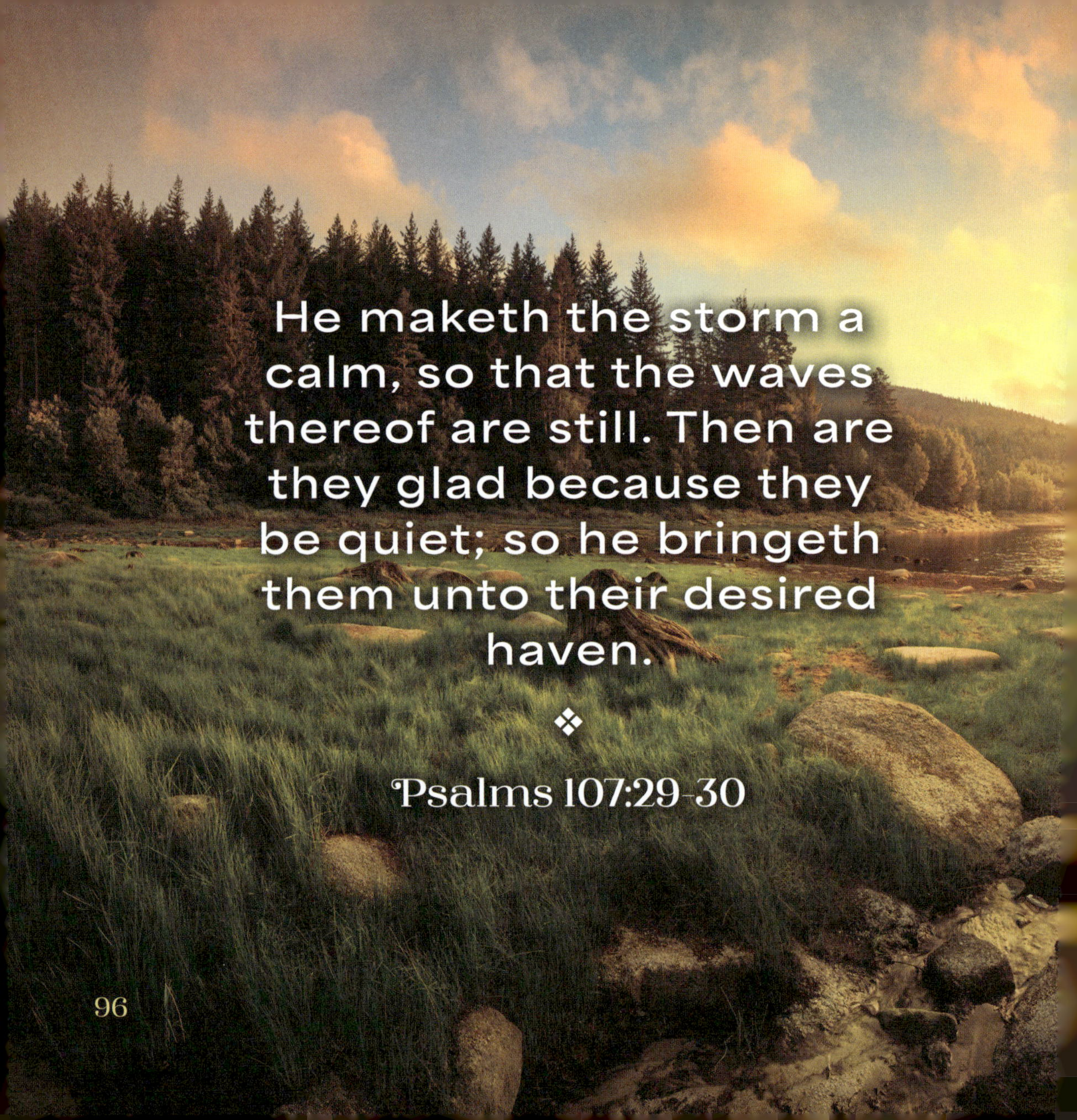

He maketh the storm a calm, so that the waves thereof are still. Then are they glad because they be quiet; so he bringeth them unto their desired haven.

❖

Psalms 107:29-30

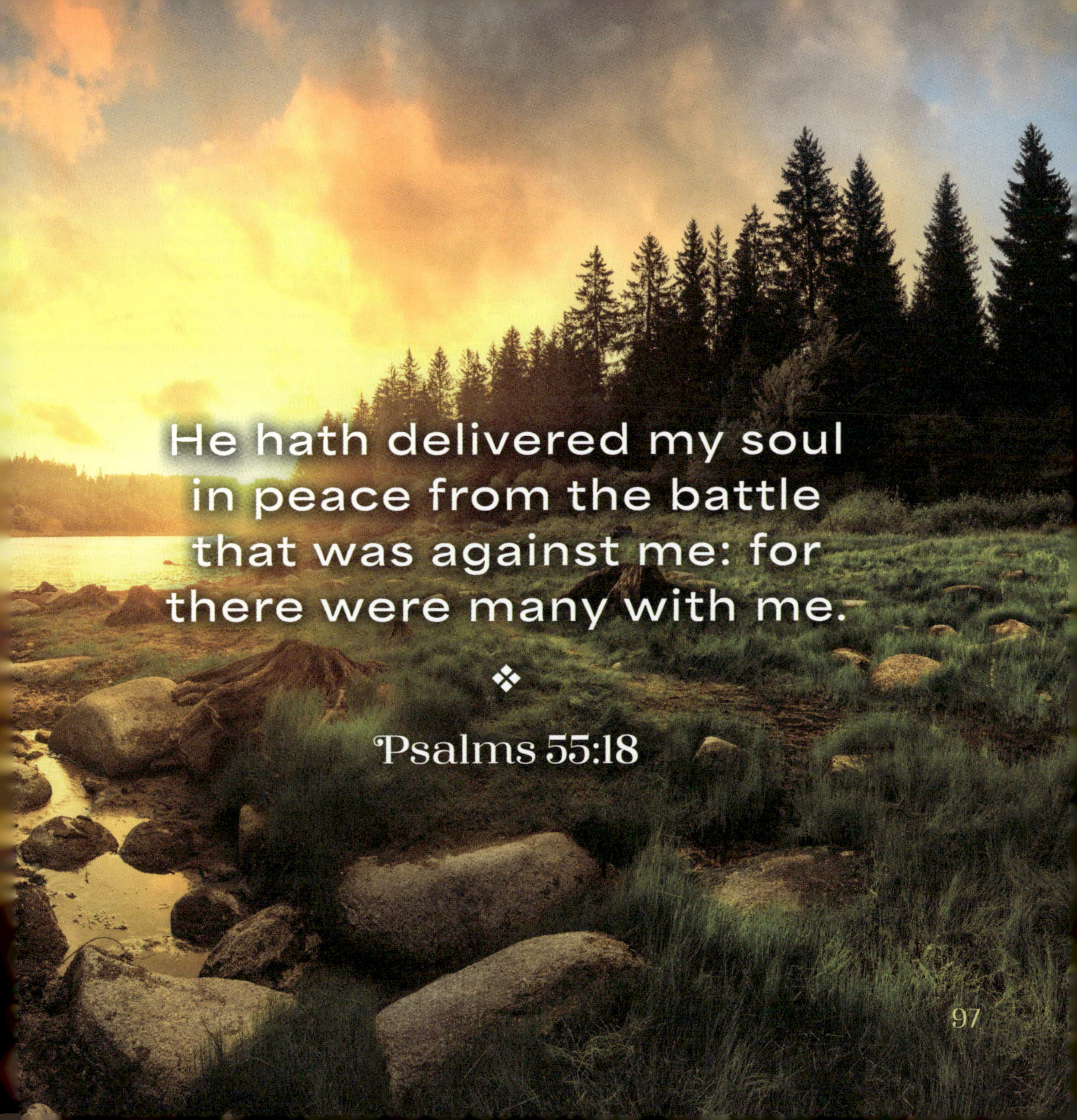

He hath delivered my soul in peace from the battle that was against me: for there were many with me.

Psalms 55:18

God's Love and the Promise of Heaven

The promise of heaven is a true testament to God's love for us. The ultimate reward for believers in Christ, heaven is a promised land filled with eternal love, eternal life, and eternal peace.

And God shall wipe away all tears from their eyes; and there shall be no more death, neither sorrow, nor crying, neither shall there be any more pain: for the former things are passed away.

Revelation 21:4

There is no greater reward to seek, no greater accolade to aspire to, than the kingdom of Heaven.

Chapter 5

Faith & Hope

The power of faith and hope cannot be underestimated, especially in turbulent times. Within God's love, you'll find a wellspring of faith and hope, if you trust in His love for you. You may not always understand God's ways, but hope can provide you with confidence, stability, and freedom from fear.

Jesus saith unto him, Thomas, because thou hast seen me, thou hast believed: blessed are they that have not seen, and yet have believed.

John 20:29

And I say unto you, Ask,
and it shall be given you;
seek, and ye shall find;
knock, and it shall be
opened unto you.

❖

Luke 11:9

And this is the confidence that we have in him, that, if we ask any thing according to his will,he heareth us.
1 John 5:14

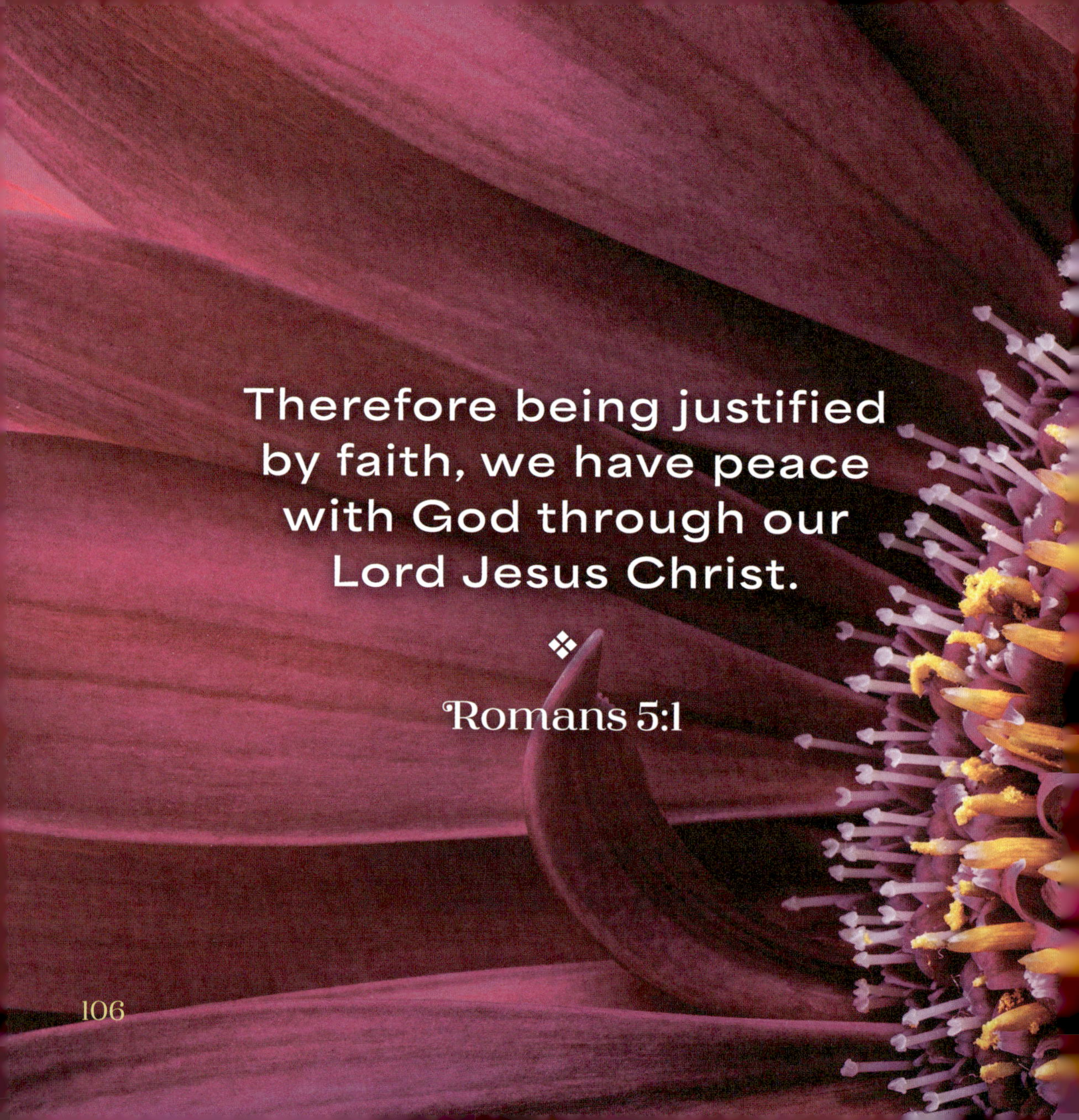

Therefore being justified by faith, we have peace with God through our Lord Jesus Christ.

❖

Romans 5:1

Trust in the Lord with all thine heart, and lean not unto thine own understanding. In all thy ways acknowledge him, and he shall direct thy paths.

❖

Proverbs 3:5-6

For the Lord shall be thy confidence, and shall keep thy foot from being taken.

❖

Proverbs 3:26

What time I am afraid, I will trust in thee. In God I will praise his word, in God have I put my trust; I will not fear what flesh can do unto me.

❖

Psalms 56:3-4

Then shalt thou walk in
thy way safely, and thy
foot shall not stumble.

Proverbs 3:23

But Jesus beheld them,
and said unto them, With
men this is impossible;
but with God all things
are possible.

❖

Matthew 19:26

Every word of God is pure: he is a shield unto them that put their trust in him.

❖

Proverbs 30:5

If I ascend up into heaven, thou art there: if I make my bed in hell, behold, thou art there. If I take the wings of the morning, and dwell in the uttermost parts of the sea; Even there shall thy hand lead me, and thy right hand shall hold me. If I say, Surely the darkness shall cover me; even the night shall be light about me.

❖

Psalms 139:8-12

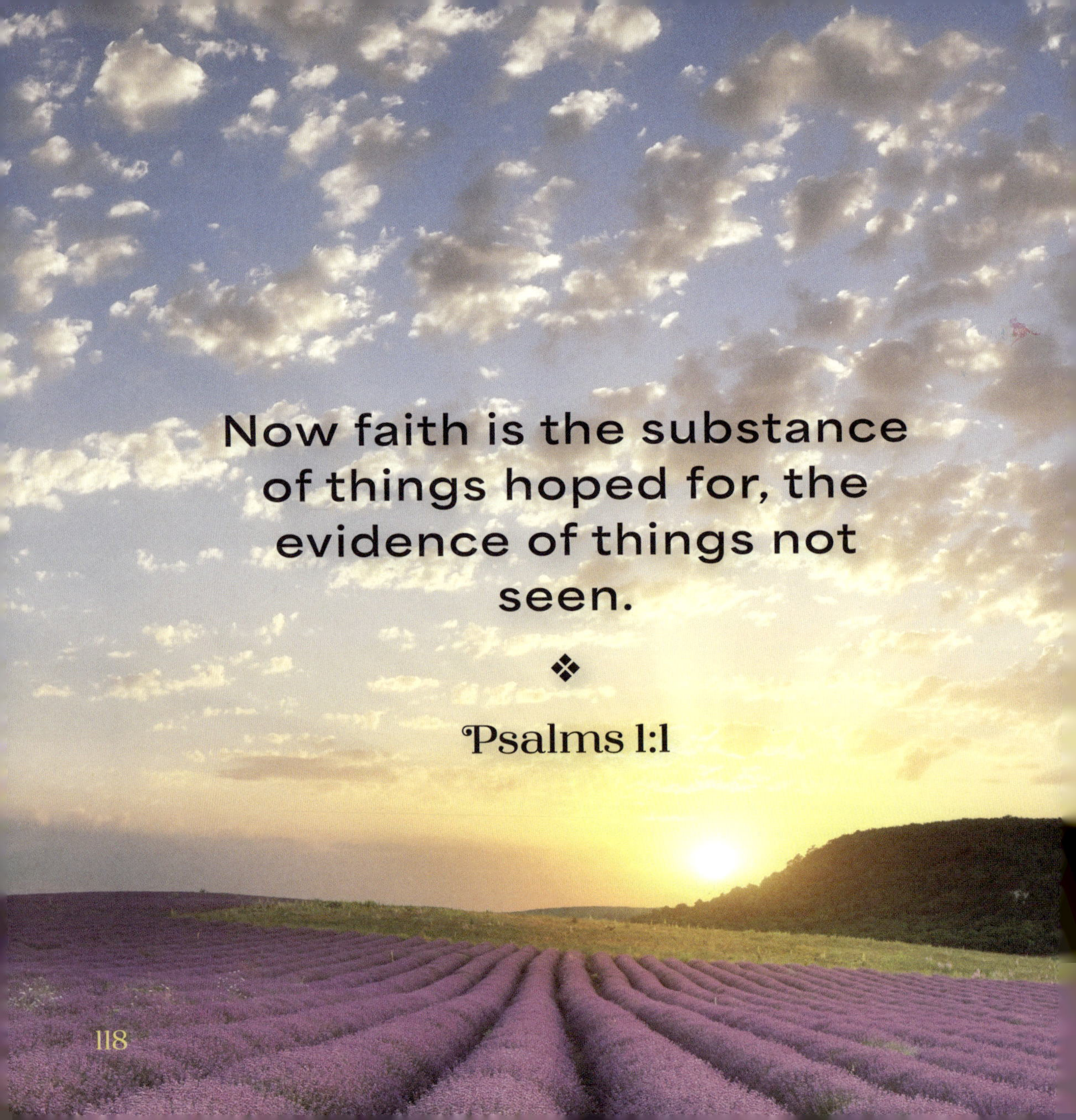

Now faith is the substance of things hoped for, the evidence of things not seen.

❖

Psalms 1:1

For we are saved by hope: but hope that is seen is not hope: for what a man seeth, why doth he yet hope for? But if we hope for that we see not, then do we with patience wait for it.

Romans 8:24-25

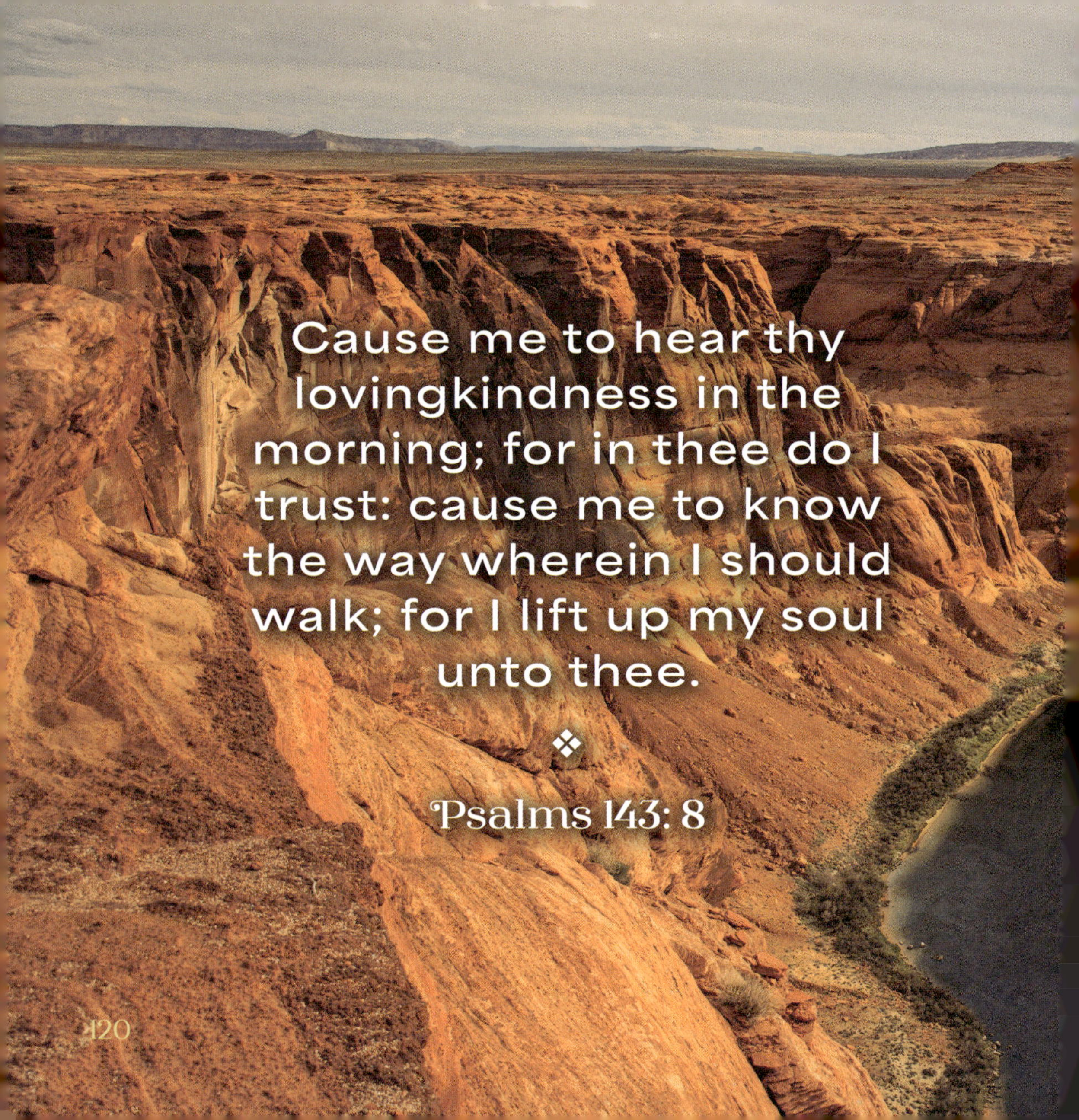

Cause me to hear thy lovingkindness in the morning; for in thee do I trust: cause me to know the way wherein I should walk; for I lift up my soul unto thee.

❖

Psalms 143: 8

The Parable of the Prodigal Son

Found in Luke, this parable tells the story of a father with two sons. His youngest son asks for his inheritance early. When he squanders that inheritance recklessly in a foreign land, he is left destitute during a famine. The son returns home, realizing his mistakes. His father welcomes him home with loving arms, compassion, and forgiveness. The older brother who has stayed home and worked obediently is resentful of his father's actions toward the youngest son.

And he answering said to his father, Lo, these many years do I serve thee, neither transgressed

I at any time thy commandment: and yet thou never gavest me a kid, that I might make merry with my friends: But as soon as this thy son was come, which hath devoured thy living with harlots, thou hast killed for him the fatted calf. And he said unto him, Son, thou art ever with me, and all that I have is thine. It was meet that we should make merry, and be glad: for this thy brother was dead, and is alive again; and was lost, and is found.

Luke 15:29-32

This parable reminds us of God's deep love and willingness to forgive, even those who have been lead astray.

Chapter 6

Strength & Comfort

God's love is the ultimate source for strength and comfort. Through His salvation, you'll find courage, guidance, patience, and more. Tribulations cannot be altogether avoided, but with God at your side, the storms are easier to fare.

Fear thou not; for I
am with thee: be not
dismayed; for I am thy
God: I will strengthen
thee; yea, I will help thee;
yea, I will uphold thee
with the right hand of my
righteousness.

❖

Isaiah 41:10

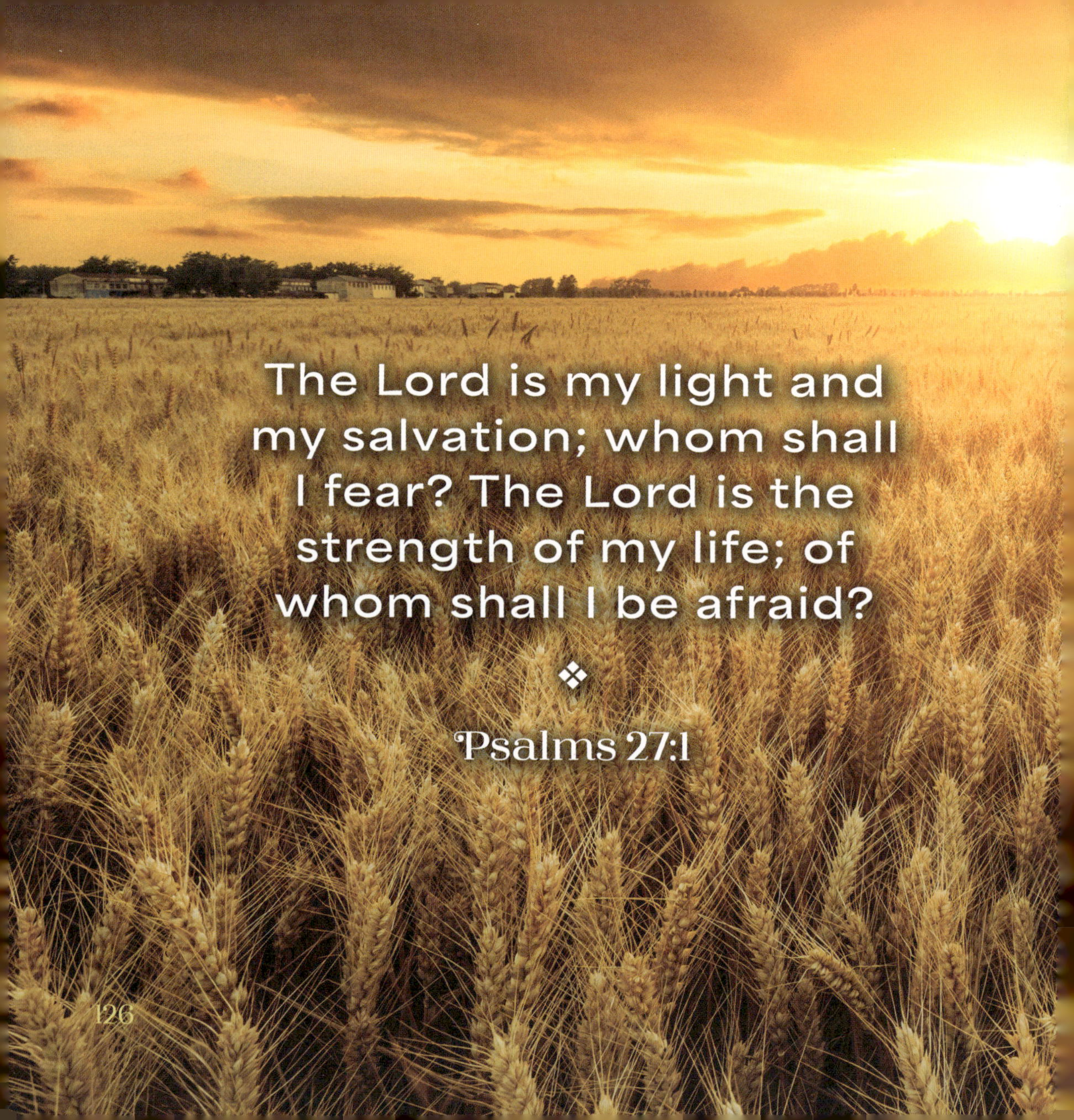
The Lord is my light and my salvation; whom shall I fear? The Lord is the strength of my life; of whom shall I be afraid?
Psalms 27:1

My flesh and my heart faileth: but God is the strength of my heart, and my portion for ever.

❖

Psalms 73:26

And I was with you in weakness, and in fear, and in much trembling. And my speech and my preaching was not with enticing words of man's wisdom, but in demonstration of the Spirit and of power: That your faith should not stand in the wisdom of men, but in the power of God.

❖

1 Corinthians 2:3-5

And not only so, but we glory in tribulations also: knowing that tribulation worketh patience; And patience, experience; and experience, hope.

Romans 5:3-4

Be strong and of a good courage, fear not, nor be afraid of them: for the Lord thy God, he it is that doth go with thee; he will not fail thee, nor forsake thee.

❖

Deuteronomy 31:6

Be of good courage, and he shall strengthen your heart, all ye that hope in the Lord.

Psalms 31:24

But the God of all grace,
who hath called us unto
his eternal glory by Christ
Jesus, after that ye have
suffered a while, make
you perfect, stablish,
strengthen, settle you.

1 Peter 5:10

But they that wait upon the Lord shall renew their strength; they shall mount up with wings as eagles; they shall run, and not be weary; and they shall walk, and not faint.

❖

Isaiah 40:31

The Lord is my strength and my shield; my heart trusted in him, and I am helped: therefore my heart greatly rejoiceth; and with my song will I praise him.

❖

Psalms 28:7

Teaching them to observe all things whatsoever I have commanded you: and, lo, I am with you always, even unto the end of the world. Amen.

Matthew 28:20

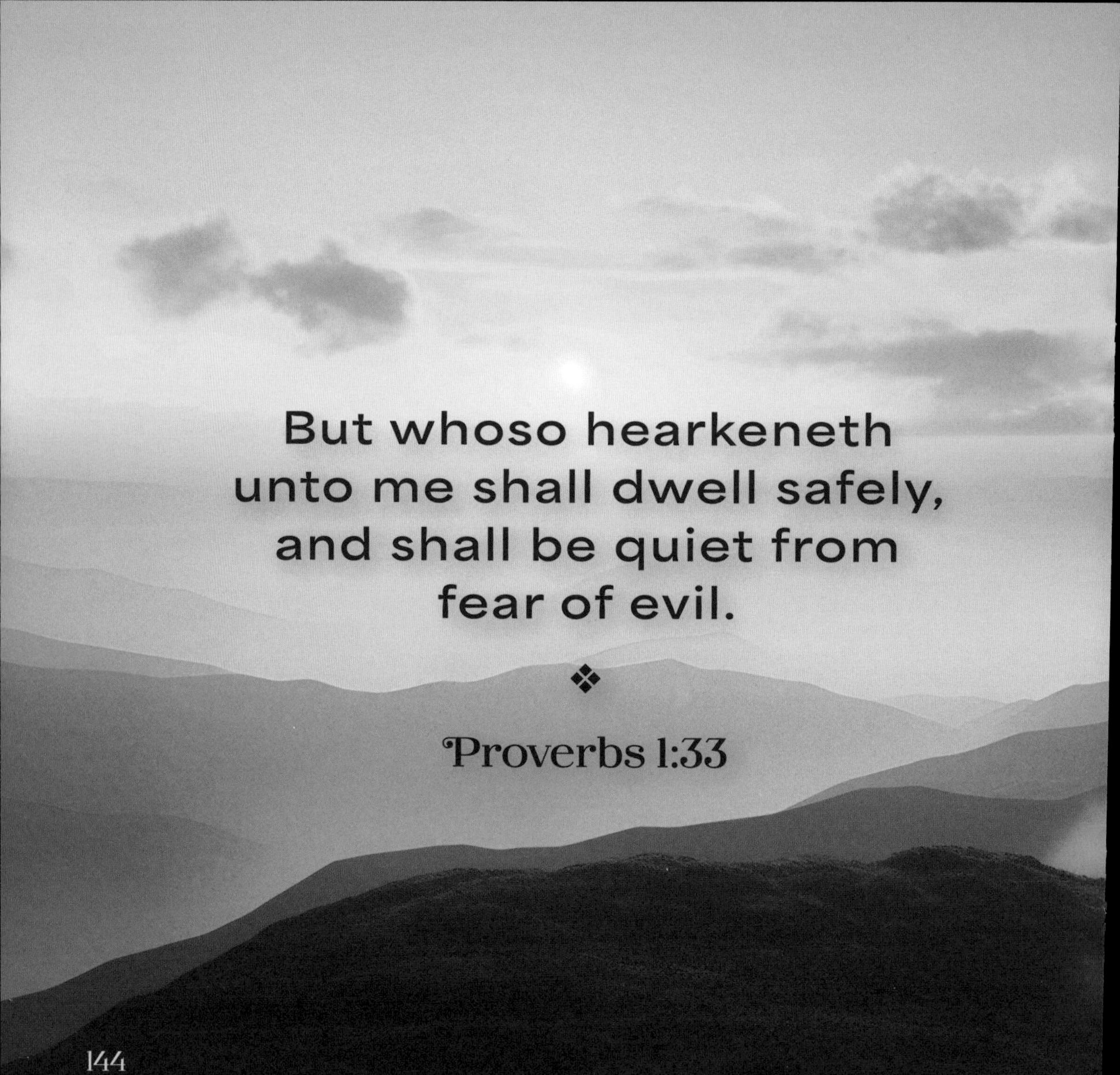

But whoso hearkeneth unto me shall dwell safely, and shall be quiet from fear of evil.

Proverbs 1:33

But the salvation of the righteous is of the Lord: he is their strength in the time of trouble.

Psalms 37:39

God is our refuge and strength, a very present help in trouble.

❖

Psalms 46:1

Have not I commanded thee? Be strong and of a good courage; be not afraid, neither be thou dismayed: for the Lord thy God is with thee whithersoever thou goest.

❖

Joshua 1:9

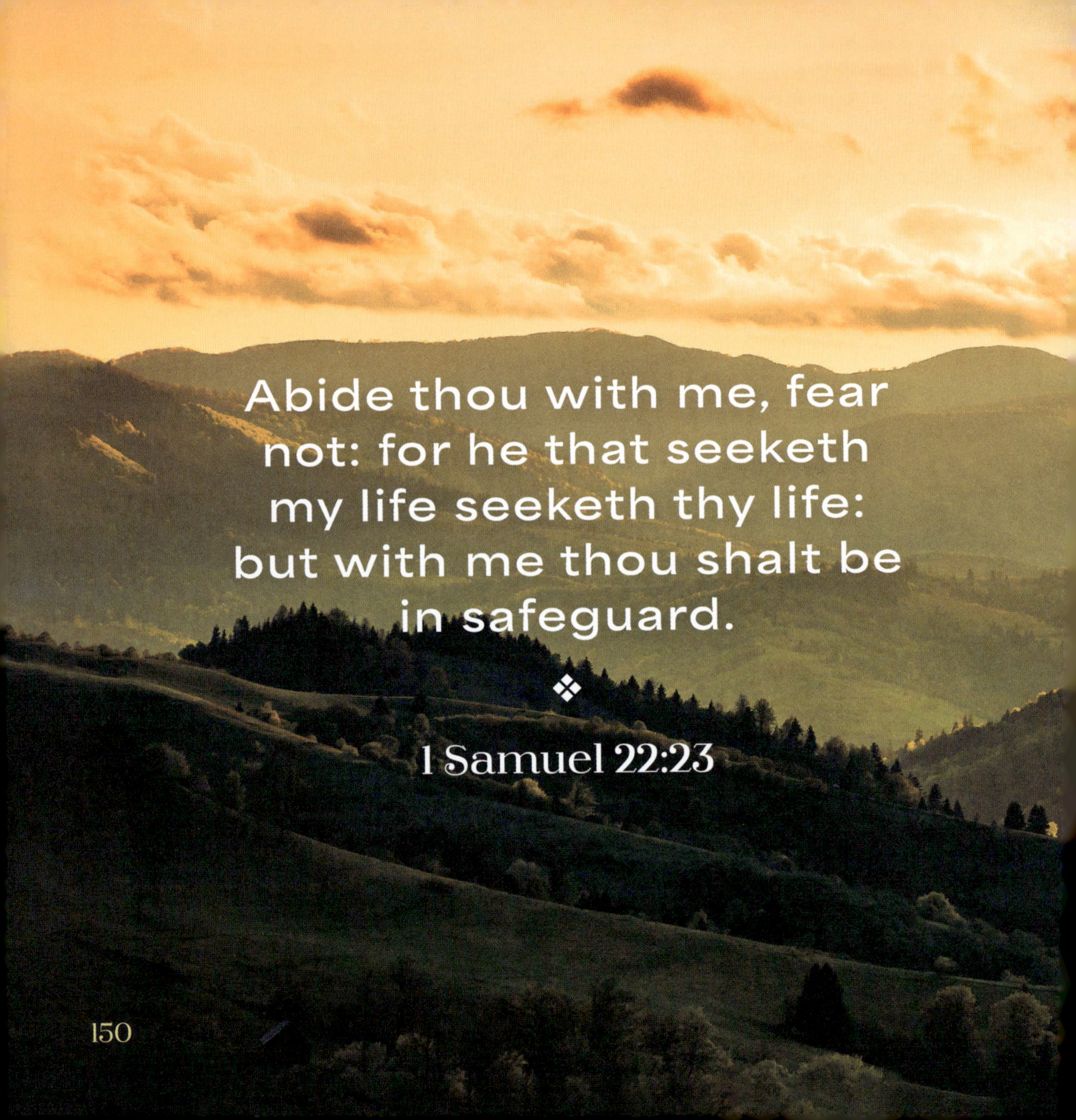

Abide thou with me, fear not: for he that seeketh my life seeketh thy life: but with me thou shalt be in safeguard.

1 Samuel 22:23

Wherefore comfort yourselves together, and edify one another, even as also ye do.

❖

1 Thessalonians 5:1

For this God is our God for ever and ever: he will be our guide even unto death.

❖

Psalms 48:14

Come unto me, all ye that labor and are heavy laden, and I will give you rest.

Matthew 11:28

God's Love and the Story of Job

God's love for us does not mean we never experience adversity. Nowhere is this better illustrated than in the story of Job. A perfect child of God, blessed, wealthy, and blameless, Job's faith is tested by Satan, who interprets Job's devotion to God as a condition of his good fortune.

After a series of hardships, deaths, and losses, Job accepts the constraints of human's understanding of God's nature, though he never loses his hope and faith in God. Finally, God intervenes, and Job is rewarded twice over.

The story of Job reminds us that when we face hardship and tragedy in life, it's okay to be sad and ask questions but ultimately we can trust that God is with us and cares about us. God will not forsake those who maintain their courage and their faith. God never stops loving us.